CLASSIC
SPORTS CARS

CLASSIC SPORTS CARS

RICHARD L. KNUDSON

PI4620

Lerner Publications Company ■ Minneapolis, Minnesota

ACKNOWLEDGMENTS: All of the photographs in this book
have been provided by the author.

LIBRARY OF CONGRESS CATALOGING IN PUBLICATION DATA

Knudson, Richard L.
  Classic sports cars.

  (Superwheels and Thrill Sports)
  SUMMARY: Introduces various classic
European and American sports cars and discusses
their development and importance in automotive
history.

  1. Sports cars—Juvenile literature. [1. Sports
cars] I. Title.

TL236.K58 1979   629.22'22   79-4641
ISBN 0-8225-0427-8

Published simultaneously in Canada by J. M. Dent & Sons
(Canada) Ltd., Don Mills, Ontario.

Manufactured in the United States of America.

International Standard Book Number: 0-8225-0427-8
Library of Congress Catalog Card Number: 79-4641

1 2 3 4 5 6 7 8 9 10 85 84 83 82 81 80 79

**The Bugatti, a classic sports car from France, has
as its trademark a horseshoe-shaped radiator.**

CONTENTS

The present-day MGB (*foreground*) differs from the 1955 TF (*background*). Both are handsome cars; one already is a classic and the other will be a classic in the future.

INTRODUCTION

Nothing on four wheels can compete with the sports car for fun, speed, and style. Sports cars are designed for the enjoyment and satisfaction of their drivers, and they combine good looks, high performance, and exact control.

Sports cars are beautiful vehicles. Usually they are two-seaters with sleek bodies built low to the ground. In the past they were always open cars, but now many closed coupes are also genuine sports cars.

Sports cars are powered by high-performance engines. Today, many popular sports cars are built with 8-cylinder engines. Some even have 12 cylinders. Most sports cars old enough to be called classics, though, were built with engines of 4 or 6 cylinders.

Sports cars have quick steering, firm suspension, and sensitive brakes. These characteristics, along with their high performance and an instrument panel that tells the driver exactly how the car is performing, let a driver feel in full control of a car at all times.

The word *classic* can describe an item that has stood the test of time and is still desirable to many people. Classic sports cars fit that definition. They are cars that were popular when they were new and remain equally popular today as cars for collectors. When they were made, these cars appealed to buyers because of their performance, beauty, precision engineering, and high quality. Few cars have all four of these characteristics. Those that do never die — they become classics.

Called "Old Number One," this was the first M.G. built for sports car events. It dates from 1925.

MIGHTY MIDGET: THE M.G.

As early as 1923, Cecil Kimber, the manager of the Morris Garages in Oxford, England, was fitting specially designed bodies to standard Morris chassis, or frames. These specials out-performed the regular Morris cars. They were sold to customers who wanted to take part in competitive events such as trials, rallies, and hillclimbs.

Cecil Kimber entered one of these cars in the 1925 London Land's End Trial, where it won a gold medal. Later Kimber always referred to that car as the first M.G. These special cars soon became a production item and were named M.G. after Morris Garages.

Because they were sporty and inexpensive, the M.G.s became very popular. By 1929, the M.G. Car Company had separated from Morris Garages and opened its own factory in Abingdon, right outside the city of Oxford.

The sight of their first M.G. has introduced sports cars to people everywhere. Today, when enthusiasts all over the world think of classic sports cars, they picture the M.G. with its familiar square radiator, long hood (the British say "bonnet" instead), and cutaway doors.

THE M TYPE MIDGET

The first M.G. sports car to be mass-produced was the M Type Midget. The M Type, introduced in 1929, was a small two-seater with a pointed-tail body. It was powered by a tiny 847 cc (cubic centimeter) engine. Before the M Type was made, only wealthy people could afford to own sports cars. Production of the M Type made it possible for the average person to own a sports car. M.G. has become the world's leading manufacturer of sports cars because it has continued to make cars of high quality at fairly low prices.

In 1930 a team of specially prepared M Types was entered in the famous Double Twelve race at Brooklands in England. This was an endurance race of 24 hours. It was run in two parts, half on one day and half on the next. The tiny M Types were matched against much larger and faster cars, but in the end they won. This established M.G. as a highly competitive motor car.

Today the M Type is prized as a classic sports car. Not many of the 3,200 produced in the years 1928 to 1932 survive, but those that do delight people everywhere.

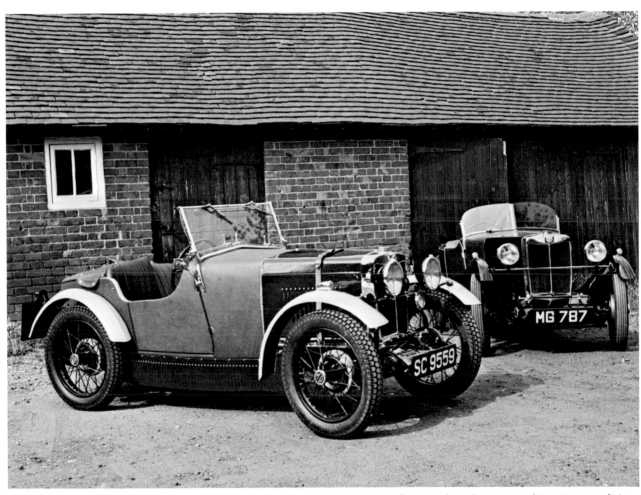

The competition M Type had an outside exhaust system, cutaway doors, a hood strap, and two-tone paint.

THE K3

During the 1930s, the M.G. became known as a leading sports car because of its success on the race courses of England and Europe. The K3 won more races than any of the other M.G.s produced during that period.

The K3 was designed as a racing car, but many owners used their K3s as road cars as well. They did this for two reasons. First, because most races of that period took place on public roads, racing cars had to be able to maintain high speeds on all kinds of surfaces, hills, and turns. The K3 could do that and still handle well. Second, the K3 looked just the way a sports/racing car should look. Out front was a massive cowling, or metal covering, which concealed a supercharger that provided a powerful boost for the 1,087-cc, six-cylinder engine. (A supercharger increases the pressure of the gasoline/air mixture.) The K3's big outside exhaust and cycle fenders helped make it the handsomest and fastest in its class.

The M.G. K3 won the team prize and was first in its class in the first race it entered — the famous Mille Miglia in Italy. Captain George Eyston and Count Johnny Lurani drove through all kinds of conditions over 1,000 miles of Italian roads to earn the 1933 victory for the M.G.

Of the 33 K3s produced in 1933 and 1934, a surprising number have survived. Even today K3s are entered in vintage sports car races all over the world, and they are still winning.

The K3 was the most successful racing M.G. Even today K3s are winning vintage car races.

THE TC

The M.G. TC is the car that started the sports car revolution in the United States. When American soldiers came home from World War II in 1945 and 1946, those who had been in England told about a car they had grown to love — the M.G. TC. Many were able to bring one home, and the TC soon became popular in the United States. Designers in Detroit noticed this; as a result, in the early 1950s the Chevrolet Corvette and two-seater Ford Thunderbird were born. American manufacturers also added such things as four-speed transmissions and quick steering to some American cars in an effort to match the performance of European sports cars.

Sports car competition in America really started after World War II when TCs were raced on the open roads of Watkins Glen, New York. Drivers in other parts of the country followed this lead, and soon road racing became very popular as a sport. Now racing is done on artificial road courses built to resemble the public roads of the old days, with many sharp corners, curves, and grades.

By winning many races, the TC established M.G., and probably all foreign cars, in the United States. Ever since the TC was introduced, foreign sports cars have claimed an important share of new car sales each year.

The TC is still the favorite of enthusiasts everywhere. It is the car that inspired the term "cornering on rails" because of the way it can take turns at high speed, much the way a train does. With its large wire wheels and sweeping fenders, it is everything a sports car should be — a perfect combination of beauty and performance.

The TC started the sports car boom in America after World War II.
It was fast and beautiful, and automobile enthusiasts loved it.

THE MGA

The MGA is just beginning to be collected as a classic sports car. When it was introduced in 1955, this car looked very different from earlier M.G.s. Gone were the traditional square grille and long sweeping fenders. This modern classic's shape was streamlined in order to lower wind resistance. People who loved the old design were unhappy at first about the new shape, but they eventually accepted this new car from Abingdon. In fact, more than 100,000 MGAs were built, so obviously some people must have liked them.

The improved shape made the MGA faster than previous M.G.s. The MGA was raced and rallied all over America. It also participated in famous international races such as the Le Mans 24-Hour Race, the Sebring

The MGA was the first streamlined M.G. Many have been destroyed by rust; those that survive are highly prized.

The dashboard (*above*) of the MGA, a right-hand drive car from England. The twin overhead camshaft engine (*below*) was used in some MGAs. It was powerful but difficult to keep tuned.

12-Hour Race, the Mille Miglia, and the Targa Florio.

One version of the MGA was produced with a twin overhead-camshaft engine. The regular MGA had a four-cylinder engine much like the engine all M.G.s had used for the previous 20 years. But the twin cam was different. It could rev (accelerate) much higher and could produce more horsepower. It was difficult to keep in tune, however, and was taken off the production line after about 2,000 had been made.

The MGA body was more apt to rust than earlier M.G.s. As a result, many rusted-out MGAs have been scrapped over the years. Because of this, those that are left have become sought-after collectors' cars.

SLEEK CAT: THE JAGUAR

The Jaguar is one of the prettiest and most expensive sports cars made. It is hard to believe that the well-known English company that makes this car began as a manufacturer of motorcycle sidecars.

Because early automobiles in England were very expensive and subject to high taxes, the motorcycle was once a widely used means of transportation. If a family man wanted to take his wife and children along on a trip, he had to have a sidecar for his motorcycle. William Lyons formed the Swallow Sidecar Company in 1922. His sidecars were well built and very popular with the customers.

The company got its start in the automobile business by building graceful bodies for a variety of chassis furnished by customers. In the early days of the automobile industry, it was a common practice to buy a chassis — a car without a body — from one company, and then to have the body built by another.

In 1931 the Swallow Sidecar Company produced its first complete car, the S.S. I. Between 1931 and 1934 this manufacturer concentrated on building complete cars and gradually eliminated its custom body division. In 1934 the name was changed to S.S. Cars Ltd., but it wasn't until the next year that the first Jaguar appeared. These first Jaguars were sedans (the British say "saloons") rather than sports cars. The company still produces a very fine, fast, sporty-looking sedan.

The fact that these first sedans were capable of high performance prompted the S.S. engineers to produce a sports car. They placed an attractive two-seater body on a shortened sedan chassis and called it the S.S. 90. This car remained in production for only a short time before it was replaced by the highly successful S.S. 100.

The Jaguar S.S. 100 is a true classic. Its flowing fenders, large wire wheels, and long hood combine to make it a beatiful sports car.

THE S.S. 100

The S.S. 100 is an excellent example of the classic sports car look. Long, sweeping fenders and big wire wheels combine to give it an appearance of power and speed. When it was introduced in 1936, this car had better performance than anything else in its class. The only car that could come close was the German BMW 328, also considered a classic sports car today.

International rallies are a popular form of sports car competition in Europe. A rally tests a car's performance and handling as well as the skills of its driver and navigator. Most manufacturers of sports cars sponsor teams of cars in these events because they know that success in competition means increased sales. The S.S. 100 was a winner in most of the important rallies in the late 1930s. It won the best performance award in the International Alpine Trial of 1936. It came in first in England's Royal Automobile Club Rally of 1937, and was first in its class in the Welsh Rally in 1937, 1938, and 1939. Success also came on the race track. One win by

Tommy Wisdom gives a good picture of the racing performance of the S.S. 100. In 1937 he won a Brooklands race at an average speed of 111 miles per hour. His fastest lap was at 117 miles per hour — not bad for a 1936 British sports car.

Like all automobile companies, Jaguar did not produce cars during World War II (1939-1945), but at the close of the war the company started designing an entirely new sports car for the world market. It is interesting to note that the letters "S.S." were dropped at this time because they reminded people of the German S.S. troups. The postwar cars were called XKs. These two letters referred to the fine engine that powered Jaguars from 1948 until the 1970s, when a 12-cyclinder model was introduced.

The famous XK twin overhead cam engine was used by Jaguar for 20 years.

The XK120 was the first streamlined Jaguar.

The D Type Jaguar was a fast and successful competition car. Many later sports cars were patterned after it.

THE XK120

The XK120 got its name because its top speed was 120 miles per hour! Introduced in 1948, it revolutionized sports car design. The XK120 was one of the first cars to demonstrate the benefits of aerodynamic design. The square front of the old S.S. 100 was replaced by a rounded wind-cutting shape that increased speed and was to become the standard design in the years ahead.

With its superior performance, the XK120 won many races and rallies all over the world. Perhaps its most impressive wins came in 1951, when an XK-engined C Type won the Le Mans 24-hour race, and in 1954, when a D Type won the same race. The D Type was designed as a racing car, although a few road-equipped versions were made in 1957. This very fast and beautiful car ran up an impressive string of victories from 1954 until 1957, when the factory withdrew from racing.

The XKE was very modern and different when it was new. Today its timelessness has made it a classic.

THE XKE

When the Jaguar XKE was introduced in 1961, the motoring press was loud in its praise. Its looks, construction, and engine all came from the D Type. It is a design that still looks modern almost 20 years after it first appeared. The XKE offered customers luxury, safety, and performance for a surprisingly low price — less than that of a Corvette, for example. The XKE was the fastest production Jaguar of all time. Its top speed was 150 miles per hour, while second gear was good for 80 miles per hour.

In racing, the XKE did not have the success its makers expected, but it proved to be competitive by placing in several important races. It attracted enthusiasts, however, as a GT (Grand Touring) car — an enclosed coupe used for long trips. The XKE was a much wanted sports car when in production and today is a perfect example of a modern classic.

ONE TO BEAT: THE BUGATTI

Ettore Bugatti was an automotive genius. He was extremely creative and could have been a famous artist had he not decided to build automobiles.

Bugatti was born in Italy in 1881 and was an active race driver in his teens. When only 18 years old, he built his first car. It won several awards at the Milan International Exhibition. Over the next few years he worked with at least two companies in the production of his designs. What he really wanted, however, was to produce his own automobile.

In 1910 Bugatti opened a factory in Molsheim, which is in eastern France. His main interest was in making competition cars. In Europe during the first half of this century, racing was done on public roads that were closed to regular traffic for the day. Bugatti's major designs were for cars that could compete in those events and also be safe, fast road cars for everyday use. Over the years Bugattis became highly successful competition cars. Some enthusiasts say that if all the victories these cars scored could be recorded, it would be clear that no other make has won so often. Whatever the case, Bugattis won more than their share of races.

The Bugatti may have won more races than any other sports car. Even today 40-year-old Bugattis are still winning races of vintage sports cars.

THE TYPE 35

The eight-cylinder Type 35 made Bugatti the car to beat between 1925 and 1932. The Type 35 had everything that makes the Bugatti a classic sports car. The horseshoe-shaped radiator, a Bugatti trademark, showed its designer's love of thoroughbreds in both horses and cars. The engine was offered in a variety of forms, supercharged and unsupercharged. It was always highly polished, as were the axles and controls. A Type 35 owner had to be a real enthusiast, because the car had neither top nor fenders, and the driver had to wear goggles in order to see at high speeds. The Type 35 was a perfect combination of racing machine and road car.

THE TYPE 43

The Type 43 has been called one of the really great Bugatti models. It first appeared in 1927 and could achieve 100 miles per hour with its four-seater open body. This car was designed for fast touring and was very successful in trials and rallies. Some later versions were closed coupes, but the typical Bugatti was an open car.

Most Bugattis were painted a lovely shade of blue. You might be tempted to call it "sky blue," but sports car enthusiasts call it "Bugatti blue." Bugatti sports cars have all become extremely rare and valuable; in fact, they are probably the most valuable of all true classic sports cars.

The Type 43 Bugatti was extremely popular. Cast aluminum wheels were a regular Bugatti feature.

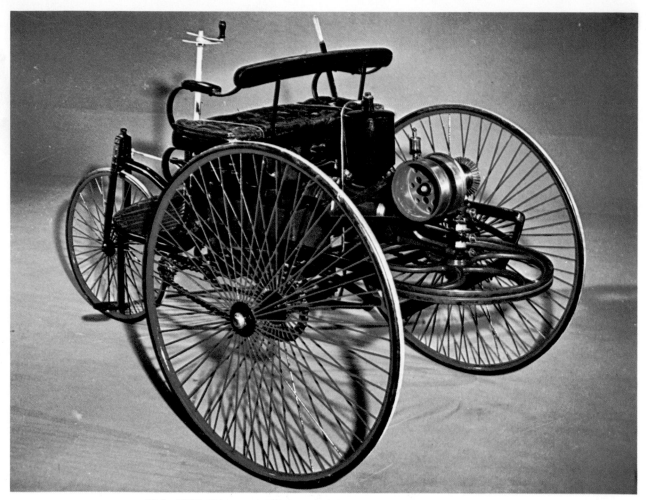

This 1886 Benz was the forerunner of today's Mercedes-Benz.
It had a simple engine in the rear and was steered with a tiller.

FAST GERMANS: MERCEDES-BENZ AND PORSCHE

Since the beginning of the industrial revolution, the German people have been noted for fine quality and precision craftsmanship in all of the goods they manufacture. This has been particularly true of sports cars produced in Germany. Mercedes-Benz and Porsche are two outstanding examples.

MERCEDES-BENZ

Mercedes-Benz can trace its history back to the very first cars. As early as 1886, Karl Benz was making cars in Mannheim, Germany. At about the same time, also in Germany, Wilhelm Maybach and Gottleib Daimler founded the Daimler Company. In 1900 they produced the first Mercedes, named after the daughter of one of its designers. Although Daimler died shortly afterward and Maybach left in 1907, the company continued to produce the Mercedes. In 1926, the Daimler and Benz firms merged and began producing the Mercedes-Benz. Two cars made by this company, the SSKL and the 300SL, stand out as examples of the classic sports car.

The Mercedes SSKL

The SSKL was an outstanding motor car. It had a powerful supercharged engine. In order to save weight, holes were drilled in the car wherever it could be done without affecting strength. The chassis, seats, pedal arms, and brake drums were all drilled for lightness. The overall weight saving was about 250 pounds, and that meant quite a bit of extra speed for racing.

The best Mercedes-Benz driver of the time was Rudi Caracciola, who won many races with the SSKL. He won the 1931 Mille

The 1927 Mercedes-Benz SSKL (*left*) produced 170 horsepower without a supercharger and 225 horsepower with the supercharger added. The external exhausts were copied by many manufacturers. The 1936 540K Mercedes (*above*) was based on the SSKL.

Miglia (the 1,000-mile race around Italy) and thus became the only German driver to accomplish that feat in a German car. He went on to win important international races at the Avus and the Nurburgring, two famous tracks in Germany.

The SSKL was the last of the Mercedes-Benz sports cars to feature the large, squarish radiator. After the 1930s, all of the company's cars were designed to cut through the air more efficiently. A good example of the new shape is the 300SL.

The 300SL was the first car to use the gullwing door—an unusual way to enter a car.

The Mercedes 300SL

During World War II, no new cars were made and automobile racing was stopped. By the end of the war, the makers of the Mercedes, like other car makers, were anxious to return to racing. They knew that winning races would help them sell passenger cars and trucks. Mercedes-Benz began racing again in 1952 with a winning automobile, the very

The 300SL, a beautiful road car, was introduced as a racing car. The opening behind the front wheels provided cooling for the brakes.

advanced 300SL. During its production life, the 300SL was offered as an open roadster and a closed coupe. The coupe was the most interesting because of gullwing doors.

"Nowhere is it written that a door can only open sideways," said Mercedes racing manager, Alfred Newbauer, who interpreted racing rules so the new design would be accepted at the various races. The doors of the 300SL opened upward, and the driver and passenger entered by stepping up and over the side of the car. When they were seated, they could pull the doors down and shut. The 300SL was very fast and comfortable. Like the SSKL, it won many races. Its most memorable victory was in the 1952 Mexican Road Race.

PORSCHE

The first cars to bear the name Porsche did not appear until the late 1940s, but Dr. Ferdinand Porsche was designing cars for many years before that. In fact, he has been called the most influential automobile designer of all time. His major contribution was the famous Volkswagen Beetle. His designs for the Porsche sports cars, however, have set the standard for all sports cars of the future.

The first pure Porsche sports car was the Type 356. Most of the final design of this car was done by Porsche's son, Ferry. The prototype, or first one made, was completed in 1948. It was based upon the then current Volkswagen, but many improvements were made to help it perform better than the Volkswagen. Also, an open two-seater body was fitted to the Volkswagen chassis. In the beginning only five cars of this kind were made each month. Today Porsche is a major manufacturer of quality sports cars.

The 356 Porsche coupe was a handsome car that established the Porsche as an excellent sports car.

In the 1970s the Porsche was offered in several versions and became extremely expensive. The 911 series still used the rear engine design made popular by Volkswagen.

The RSK Porsche was a racing version that had considerable success in America and Europe.

The engine of the Porsche 356, like that of the Volkswagen was in the rear. All of the early Porsches had flat, air-cooled, horizontally-opposed, four-cylinder engines that were very different from the water-cooled, vertical cylinder engines earlier cars had used. They were designed for peak efficiency in air flow. The perfect combination of shape, weight, and power meant that the car was capable of very high performance.

The first major race for the 356 was the 1951 Le Mans 24-hour race. Driven by two Frenchmen, Veuillet and Mouche, the only Porsche entered won its class easily. This win established the Porsche as an outstanding competitor.

The 356 remained in production for 20 years, and was the sort of car that other manufacturers tried to copy. The 356 was known for its outstanding handling, smooth transmission, and high quality. All of the later Porsches have the same reputation.

CLASS GLASS: THE CORVETTE

Chevrolet knew what it was doing when it introduced a sports car in 1953. By that time there were enough M.G.s, Porsches, and Jaguars buzzing around on American highways to make Detroit take notice. The Corvette was Chevrolet's answer to the Europeans. Today it is still the only true sports car made in the United States.

The only real difference between the first Corvette and other Chevrolets was a body made of fiberglass, the same material used on today's Corvettes. The engineers at General Motors chose fiberglass because by using it they could produce the car quickly. They felt, too, that this different material would be good for sales. Fiberglass also kept Corvettes

rust-free, and that meant future restorations would be easier for collectors.

The first Corvettes were two-seater roadsters. Except for their appearance, though, their right to be called true sports cars is questionable. They looked like sports cars, but their handling qualities were no better than those of any family sedan produced by Chevrolet at the time. Performance was poor even though a big six-cylinder engine provided the power. On top of everything else, the only transmission available was the Powerglide automatic — unheard of in a true sports car! In spite of all these faults, the 1953 and 1954 Corvettes are sought after today as collectable sports cars. Their right

The 1954 Corvette has become a classic sports car because it was one of the first Corvettes made. Over the years the Corvette has become a highly respected sports car.

Zora Arkus-Duntov is seated in the experimental S.S. Corvette. This car resembled the D Type Jaguar.

to classic status comes from their shape, the use of fiberglass, and the fact that the Corvette is the only American-made sports car. The first of the line, then, is entitled to be called a classic even if it lacks the performance and handling to match its looks.

The Corvette did not become a true sports car until Zora Arkus-Duntov, a talented engineer from Europe with years of sports car experience, came to work on the project.

Under his leadership the Corvette was given a new V-8 engine in 1955. He encouraged racing, so in 1956 several races were entered with some success. Because Zora Arkus-Duntov was always looking to the future, under his leadership the Corvette eventually became one of the world's leading sports cars.

In the mid-1950s the most important car in sports car racing was the D Type Jaguar. So Corvette engineers bought a D Type to study

This experimental Wankel-powered rear engine Corvette shows what future designs may look like. Will this be the classic sports car of 2050?

closely. Its influence can be seen in the handsome SS Corvette. The success of the SS led to the development of the Sting Ray line, which is quite popular with collectors.

The first Sting Ray appeared in 1963 in both roadster and coupe versions. The coupe version produced in 1963, 1964, and 1965 is very desirable today. By the time the Corvette had reached this stage of development, it was well known as a leading sports car. Good looks, performance, and quality all combined to make it a fine automobile. The V-8 engine continued to power the Corvette, and the optional fuel-injection feature added to its performance capabilities. Over the years the Corvette's handling improved to the point where it could compete with most foreign cars. When four-wheel disc brakes were introduced in 1965, the Corvette's ability to stop quickly finally matched its handling ability and speed. (Disc brakes, which use a set of clamps to grasp a rotating disc, are superior to drum brakes because heat from the braking action increases the brakes' efficiency.)

In 1968 Corvette made a major styling change, although it was not really a futuristic one. In fact, the new Corvette looked much like some of the older Ferraris. Enthusiasts had hoped that it would have a mid-engine design much like the Wankle-engine dream car that Corvette makes had been displaying at the auto shows. In spite of this disappointment, the new car was accepted and sold well. Corvette fans are convinced that the next design will bring together all the great ideas that have appeared on the Corvettes of the past. Whatever the future holds, we know that the Corvettes of the '50s and '60s have earned the right to be called classic sports cars.

The 1963 Corvette is now sought after by collectors. Not many Corvettes are made each year, and their scarcity helps to make them collectibles.

TODAY'S SPORTS CARS: TOMORROW'S CLASSICS

If we only knew which of today's cars will be the classics of tomorrow, we could put some of them away in a barn and have a valuable collection in 20 years. Predictions are always difficult. But if we base our forecasts on what we know about the classic sports cars of today, perhaps we can pick the cars that will be collectable 20 years from now.

A major concern, of course, is that a car must last for 20 years. If it has rusted away into a pile of dust, no one will want it. Because of today's *monocoque* (MAH-nah-kok),

or unibody, construction and the use of thinner steel, cars are much more apt to be victims of rust than in the past. For instance, more than half a million MGBs, M.G.'s current car, will be produced before a new M.G. is introduced, but most of those cars will be destroyed by rust. Those that survive will have a place on the classics lists of the future. The M.G. Midget is another car that will appeal to collectors 20 years from now. Both of these M.G.s have the same classic characteristics that their distinguished predecessors had.

Any of these M.G.s will be collectors' items in the future. They are good sports
cars and those that are well cared for will be show cars 20 years from now.

The Triumph TR-7 may be a collectible in 20 years because it brought the wedge shape to popular and inexpensive sports cars.

The Triumph TR-7 will probably make the lists because it was one of the first low-cost, wedge-shaped cars to appear in the 1970s. Before the introduction of the TR-7, this modern shape was available only on very expensive cars like the Ferrari. In addition to its shape, the TR-7 had excellent performance and handling qualities to its credit as well as some impressive competition activity.

Two cars which compete with each other in performance, price, and looks are the Datsun 240-Z and the Porsche 924. These

The 924 is Porsche's first front engine car. It is fast, well-designed, and bound to be a future classic.

two Grand Touring coupes have attracted very loyal owners. We know that if such loyalty exists when a car is in current production, the same sort of enthusiasm will exist among the cars' owners in the future. Both the Datsun and the Porsche will probably be show pieces at classic sports car meetings 20 years from now.

A car that is both reasonably priced and revolutionary at the time of its introduction is bound to be wanted by collectors 20 years later. The Mazda RX-7 meets these qualifications. When introduced in 1978, it was enthusiastically received by motoring writers because it had a modern look, was well-engineered, and was powered by a very different engine.

The power in the RX-7 is provided by a rotary engine named after its inventor, Felix Wankel. The Wankel engine differs from the normal cylinder-type internal combustion engine because neither pistons nor cylinders are used. It still works, however, on the same four-stroke power principle — intake, compression, power, exhaust.

When the RX-7 was introduced, its main competition on the sports car market came from such cars as Datsun 280-Z, Porsche 924, Corvette, Triumph TR-7, and the MGB. The RX-7 proved to offer more performance and styling per dollar than did any of the other

The Mazda RX-7 was assured classic status when introduced because it combined advanced ideas with beauty and performance.

cars. Because it has a top speed of over 120 miles per hour, we know that the RX-7 is a high performance car. It has excellent handling and is well-engineered throughout. It has beauty and high quality. Most important, however, is the fact that it was the first mass-produced rotary-engine sports car. The RX-7 is destined for an initial career as a very competitive sports car and can look forward to retirement years as a desirable classic.

Another contemporary sports car, the amazing Bricklin, is already highly prized by collectors. In 20 years it is apt to be the star of every old car show. Named after its designer, Malcolm Bricklin, this unique car was produced during 1974 and 1975 in the Canadian province of New Brunswick. What made it unique? Well, its fiberglass coupe body and handsome gullwing doors (like those of the Mercedes 300SL) combined to make a beautiful shape. Further, it was designed for maximum safety with a solid frame to protect its occupants. Most of the cars used a Ford engine. Unfortunately, building cars costs a lot of money, and the Bricklin's makers ran out of funds before all of the problems were worked out. When they went out of business in 1975, fewer than 3,000 cars had been produced. The combination of rarity and unique design means that lovers of classic sports cars will be wanting the Bricklin 20 years from now.

The Bricklin was made in Canada during 1974 and 1975. It had a gullwing door like the Mercedes 300SL. Bricklins are already selling for more than they cost when new.

The M Type Midget

What makes a sports car classic? First of all, it has to stand the test of time. In addition, it must have outstanding performance, styling, and engineering qualities. It must be the sort of car that people prize when it is new and restore and care for when it is old. It must inspire admiration and enthusiasm. But above all, to achieve classic status, a sports car must continue to make driving a satisfying and enjoyable experience. A sports car that meets all of these qualifications will make its owner proud and happy for many years.

Special edition cars are instant classics. This Jubilee MGB/GT with special wheels and gold stripes was produced to celebrate M.G.'s 50th anniversary in 1976.

Superwheels & Thrill Sports

Lerner Publications Company
241 First Avenue North, Minneapolis, Minnesota 55401